FINANCES

Biblical Affirmations

OYENIKE ADETOYE   ACMA, CGMA

This book is designed to provide information and reveal some hidden secrets about biblical faith and personal finance.

It is sold with the understanding that neither the author nor the publisher is engaged in rendering legal, accounting, or other professional services by publishing this book.

As each situation is unique, questions relevant to personal finances and specific to the individual should be addressed to an appropriate professional to ensure that the situation has been evaluated carefully and appropriately.

The Author and Publisher specifically disclaim any liability, loss, or risk which is incurred as a consequence, directly or indirectly, of the use and application of the contents of this work.

Every affirmation listed in this book has a scripture, a thought to consider, and an encouragement on various topics related to wealth and money management from the Word of God. I trust God that the pages of this book will be a blessing to you, even as it has been a blessing to me while writing it.

OTHER BOOKS BY OYENIKE ADETOYE

❖ NonSecrets of the Financially Secure – Volume 1

❖ NonSecrets of the Financially Secure – Volume 2

❖ NonSecrets of the Financially Secure – Volume 3

❖ NonSecrets of the Financially Secure – Volume 4

❖ NonSecrets of the Financially Secure – Volume 5

❖ Praying for your Finances

❖ Financial Nakedness

❖ Financially Smart Teens & Young Adults

❖ The Beauty of Compounding

❖ The Four Letter Word D E B T

❖ Financial Boundaries

❖ Finances Biblical Affirmations

❖ Financial Success Quenchers

Dedication

This book is dedicated to the Most High God!

Acknowledgements

To God who inspired the writing of this book.

To my darling husband and beautiful daughters, for cheering me on while I spent late nights and early mornings working on this book.

To my amazing siblings, for being a strong support and encouragement on this journey.

To everyone that has supported my dreams and inspired me to keep writing.

Thank you so much!

Oyenike.

Contents

"You will have to live with the consequences of everything you say. What you say can preserve life or destroy it; so you must accept the consequences of your words."

— **Proverbs 18:20-21 GNT**

About This Book

This book is a great spiritual tool for serious-minded believers who are cultivating a biblical lifestyle of trusting God for their finances.

I have grouped this book into sections for ease of reading. I used the acronym **'MMM'** - which stands for 'Making Money', 'Managing Money', and 'Multiplying Money', for the grouping. The first section covers the biblical affirmations on Making Money. Part Two of this book focuses on the biblical affirmations on Managing Money. And the last section, Part Three, covers affirmations on Multiplying Money.

The value of this book is not found in the offer of some theories about affirmation. The real power of the book is that it has been written by someone who, for the majority of her Christian life, wholeheartedly believes and confesses biblical affirmations as a way of life. She has personally experienced and enjoyed the power of God in the area of her finances, and she can boldly testify that God's ears are opened to our decrees and declarations when we do it in faith (Job 22:28).

The book of Proverbs Chapter 18 verse 21 says, "Death and life are in the power of the tongue, and those who love it and indulge it will eat its fruit and bear the consequences of their words" (Amplified Bible). This verse means that you can either bring forth good or bad by the way you use your tongue. You can literally change your life by changing the quality of your speech. When you do this, you refresh your mind and become open to the miraculous to start happening in your life.

When it comes to our finances, speaking out positive affirmations is a game-changer. We all have the God-given right to be financially free. But with all the hardships so often faced, it is easy to forget that and fall into the trap of negativity or lost hope. It is important to know that we, as God's children, can enjoy a life of more-than-enough, where bills are paid in full each month, where we are debt-free, and where we enjoy financial abundance.

Whether we realise it or not, through affirmations, we deliberately affect our subconscious mind into believing that what we are affirming is true. And the best part is that our subconscious mind will do anything possible for us to experience even more of what we are affirming. Our beliefs, inner thoughts, and dialogues are going to create our reality!

You will be amazed at how biblical money affirmations can eliminate financial insecurity and doubt. And even more, declaring positive financial affirmations will help you escape negative money patterns that keep you stuck in poverty. Biblical financial affirmations are a great way for putting a stop to the poverty mindset and completely shift to the opposite direction of abundance and financial freedom. The goal of affirmation is not to replace essential daily habits, but to instead change our mindset and get us thinking positively, no matter the situation we are in.

God called the universe into being before it ever existed. God had a vision for the world before it ever happened. You and I, being created in God's image and likeness can do the same thing. When we are affirming, we declare the things that may not yet be apparent, and we create a future reality that aligns with the truth of God's word.

Introduction

Affirmations in this book are short statements that are intentionally declared over yourself or a situation. They are powerful statements that help your mind speak positive thoughts into existence. Financial affirmations are short phrases you say to yourself about money. Your affirmations about money significantly affect your mindset, your financial decisions and consequently your financial stability.

I personally live and breathe biblical affirmations over my finances, and I can confidently tell you that they work. They are based on God's word and not my own words. God's word is the truth, and it is powerful, effective, and full of God's wonderful promises. His promises are sure, they are "YEA" and "AMEN" (2 Corinthians 1:20). Heaven and earth will pass away, but His words will never pass away (Luke 21:33).

Consistently confessing and professing biblical affirmation will help you speak biblical truth into existence. You can change your life by simply changing your words. Getting your brain and heart to connect to what you are saying with your mouth is crucial. And as you consistently do this, you will start to see your behaviour and habits towards your finances change for the better. You will start to experience a powerful shift in your mindset and beliefs about money and wealth.

Biblical affirmation should not be done occasionally. They are supposed to be part of our daily life as believers to declare them anywhere and every day. Read them out loud as many times as possible. Consistently say them over and over again until you eventually begin to believe them. Let them take charge of your thoughts, and before you know it, they will slowly increase your faith in God in the many areas of your finances, which you are trusting Him for.

I love the power of visualisation. While I was working on my debt several years ago, I had biblical money affirmations strategically put in corners around my house where I could easily see them. Seeing positive words like these, *"All my bills are paid, all my debts are settled. I owe no man nothing except for love, I am a lender to nations and not a borrower...",* several times during the day was powerful. I encourage you to do the same. Write them out. Stick them on the fridge. Stick them on a wall in your living room. Memorise the bible verse the affirmation was inspired by. And watch how this awesome biblical tool stimulates the subconscious to act on your behalf and use its enormous power to create the life you want.

I must stress the importance of taking action. Action separates dreamers from achievers. Although rooted in the power of intention, affirmations require inspired action to be effective. Voicing affirmations of what you will do or become without putting things into action is like practising faith without putting in the work; the end result is dead (James 2:17). Using the example of my debt-free journey, I was declaring, professing and confessing biblical affirmations, but I also had an action plan. I put in the hours and worked hard to increase my income, I significantly reduced my expenses, I proactively used the debt-snowball strategy, and I intentionally stopped adding new debt to my pot. The result of this powerful combo is the testimony I live by today – that I am DEBT FREE!

In case you are wondering who I am to be offering you advice about your personal finance. I am a qualified Chartered Management Accountant professional who has experienced fiscal highs and lows, been in and out of debt and has worked in various multinational FTSE 100 companies in the United Kingdom for many years. I founded LifTED Financial Consulting Ltd as a result of my personal discoveries and experiences with money on my journey to financial freedom.

Fasten your seat belt and let's get started on this journey of obtaining what is financially rightfully ours via repeatedly affirming God's word. I look forward to hearing your testimonies as you read this book.

Blessings your way!

---------Disclaimers---------

I am not a CPA, attorney, insurance, or financial advisor, and the information in this book shall not be construed as tax, legal, insurance, or financial advice. If you need such advice, please contact a qualified CPA, attorney, insurance agent, or financial advisor.

PART 1:

'MAKING MONEY' AFFIRMATIONS

I Am Grateful!

"In every situation, no matter what the circumstances, be thankful and continually give thanks to God; for this is the will of God for you in Christ Jesus."

- 1 Thessalonians 5:18 AMP

Affirmations:

I am grateful for my current financial situation. I am grateful for the financial blessings I enjoy.

I am grateful for all riches that life offers me. I am grateful for the financial abundance I experience.

I am grateful for many things in my life that bring me joy and comfort.

I am grateful to be able to count my blessings every day. I am grateful for financial freedom.

AMEN.

"A faithful man will abound with blessings, but whoever hastens to be rich will not go unpunished."

- Proverbs 28:20 ESV

Affirmations:

I am a blessed child of God. I abound with blessings.

I am a wealthy child of a wealthy and loving heavenly Father. My Father owns it all.

I am blessed and enriched daily. I always have enough money. God is my source.

I am successful, wealthy, and healthy. I am wealthy beyond my wildest dreams.

All things are mine. I radiate prosperity, money, and wealth.

AMEN.

I Have Creative Ideas!

"Do you see a man skilful in his work? He will stand before kings; he will not stand before obscure men."

- Proverbs 22:29 ESV

<u>Affirmations:</u>

My gifts and talents prosper me. I have great creative potential.

My money-making skills are growing. I have creative ideas and wealth-generation skills.

I get God-inspired ideas that produce great wealth. I have an infinite amount of inventiveness.

My creative ideas generate tons of money for me. My imagination knows no bounds.

I am a creative child of the living God. Creativity is in my DNA.

AMEN.

I Am Equipped
To Make More
Money!

*"Nations will come to your light,
And kings to the brightness of your
rising."*

- Isaiah 60:3 AMP

Affirmations:

I believe in my ability to earn more money. I believe in myself.

There is no limit to what I can earn. I will be incredibly wealthy.

Opportunities to make more money are coming my way. My income exceeds my expenses.

I deserve the opportunity to negotiate a better salary. I will be paid a fair wage for my skillset.

My income grows daily by me doing the things I love and enjoy doing. I am blessed.

AMEN.

All My Labour
Produces
Profit!

"In all labour there is profit,
But mere talk leads only to poverty."

- Proverbs 14:23 AMP

Affirmations:

Today is rich with opportunities. I open my heart to receive them.

I work when I want, where I want, with people I want to work with. God blesses the work of my hands and teaches me to profit.

Lucrative opportunities to make wealth always come my way. My capacity daily expands.

I trust my ever-increasing ability to create abundance. All my labour produces profit. Wealth and riches are in my house.

AMEN.

My Financial Income Is Increasing!

"May the favour of the Lord our God rest on us; establish the work of our hands for us - yes, establish the work of our hands."

- Psalm 90:17 NIV

Affirmations:

My financial income increases as the blessings of God take over me.

The influence of God's abundance in my life is huge. New opportunities to increase my income are opening for me.

My money is working for me to multiply my abundance. I have plenty of goods, an increase in stocks, and an increase in the produce of my businesses.

I am increasing more and more. I increase and never decrease.

AMEN.

My Net Worth
Is Increasing!

"But the path of the righteous is like the light of dawn, which shines brighter and brighter until full day."

- Proverbs 4:18 ESV

<u>Affirmations:</u>

My net worth is increasing. My wealth is increasing. God lavishly gives me all things to enjoy. I am blessed.

My assets and the things I own are increasing. My liabilities and the things I owe are decreasing.

My income is increasing. I prosper wherever I turn. My prosperity is unlimited.

Surely, God's goodness and mercy follow me all the days of my life. I always have more than enough money.

AMEN.

I Am A Successful Entrepreneur!

"Whatever you do, work at it with all your heart, as working for the Lord, not for human masters, since you know that you will receive an inheritance from the Lord as a reward. It is the Lord Christ you are serving."

– Colossians 3:23-24 NIV

Affirmations:

I am a successful and wealthy Entrepreneur.

I create wonderful business opportunities every day. I love the freedom my business produces for me.

Lucrative opportunities and resources are heading my way. My business is thriving not just surviving.

I am driven by passion and purpose. I attract great entrepreneurial opportunities. I am blessed and highly favoured.

AMEN.

I Am Blessed With Perfect Health!

"And it is a good thing to receive wealth from God and the good health to enjoy it. To enjoy your work and accept your lot in life, this is indeed a gift from God."

- Ecclesiastes 5:19 NLT

Affirmations:

I am blessed with perfectly good health to earn a living. My body is strong and capable.

I am an energetic being full of life and vitality. The Lord has blessed me with the power to make wealth.

Every part of my body and mind works perfectly in harmony, just as the Lord has created me.

I received abundant wealth from God and good health to enjoy it. Perfect health is mine.

AMEN.

God's Favour Surrounds Me!

"For the Lord God is a sun and shield; the Lord bestows favour and honour. No good thing does he withhold from those who walk uprightly."

- Psalms 84:11 ESV

Affirmations:

God's favour surrounds me. I have sufficiency in all things. I abound in every good work.

I am promoted. I am singled out for favour. I am in a season of upliftment. My life is engulfed in the aroma of God's favour.

I am blessed with favour from God and favour from men. I am blessed with the kindness of God and the kindness of men.

I am favoured above the rest. My head is exalted like the horn of a unicorn. I am specially anointed.

AMEN.

I Give Myself Permission To Prosper!

"Therefore become imitators of God, copy Him and follow His example, as well-beloved children imitate their father."

- Ephesians 5:1 AMP

Affirmations:

I give myself permission to prosper. Prosperity is mine and my prosperity is unlimited.

I see prosperity everywhere. Prosperity is my birthright.

Prosperity is within me, it is around me, it flows to me, and it flows through me. I enjoy my prosperity and share it freely with the world.

I let go of all resistance to prosperity. I create prosperity easily and effortlessly.

AMEN.

I Am Worthy Of Wealth!

"Let them shout for joy, and be glad, that favour my righteous cause: yea, let them say continually, Let the LORD be magnified, which hath pleasure in the prosperity of his servant."

- Psalm 35:27 KJV

Affirmations:

I give myself permission to make wealth. I am worthy of wealth.

I deserve to be wealthy. God created me to live in abundance.

I work every day for my financial abundance. I am deserving and worthy of success.

I am worthy of earning large amounts of money. I believe in myself.

I deserve to live comfortably and financially free. I am prosperous.

AMEN.

I Have Unstoppable Confidence!

"But blessed is the one who trusts in the Lord, whose confidence is in him."

- Jeremiah 17:7 NIV

<u>Affirmations:</u>

I have unstoppable confidence in my ability to grow wealth.

I daily use my confidence and positive attitude to create a wonderful financial situation for myself.

I have the attitude and the aptitude to reach unlimited levels of financial success.

I am capable and ready to make large amounts of money. My capacity to make and grow money daily expands.

AMEN.

I Am A Faithful Steward!

"This is how one should regard us, as servants of Christ and stewards of the mysteries of God. Moreover, it is required of stewards that they be found faithful."

- 1 Corinthians 4:1-2 ESV

Affirmations:

I am a faithful and wise steward of my God-given wealth.

I oversee God's possessions and His affairs with integrity.

All my financial possession belongs to God. He owns it all.

I am rich in good deeds and I am a generous giver.

Money is my servant. I control it by telling it what to do. I direct it by telling it where to go.

AMEN.

I Am Financially Secure!

"The good man's children will be powerful in the land; his descendants will be blessed. His family will be wealthy and rich, and he will be prosperous forever."

- Psalm 112:2-3 GNT

Affirmations:

I acquire wealth in miraculous ways. I have multiple lucrative income streams.

I have enough passive income to pay for the lifestyle I want. I am capable of building the wealth I desire.

I am well paid for my work. The more value I contribute, the more money I make.

I am able to continually multiply my money. I am financially secure.

AMEN.

PART 2:

'MANAGING MONEY' AFFIRMATIONS

I Give Thanks!

"Give thanks in all circumstances; for this is God's will for you in Christ Jesus."

- 1 Thessalonians 5:18 NIV

Affirmations:

I give thanks for the complete, immediate payment of all financial obligations. I pay all my bills with gratitude.

I give thanks that the prosperity which is mine by divine right. I am rich, wealthy, and happy.

I give thanks that I am healthy and wealthy knowing fully well that my financial affairs are in divine order.

I thank God for divine prosperity.

AMEN.

I Serve God, Not Money!

"For the love of money is a root of all kinds of evil. Some people, eager for money, have wandered from the faith and pierced themselves with many griefs."

- 1 Timothy 6:10 NIV

<u>Affirmations:</u>

I serve God, not money. I put my trust in God, not money.

I obey and serve God; I spend my days in prosperity and my years in pleasure.

I keep myself free from the love of money. Money is my servant.

God has made all grace to abound towards me. I have sufficiency in all things.

I am satisfied because the Lord has given me richly all things to enjoy.

AMEN.

I Am Financially Disciplined!

"No discipline seems pleasant at the time, but painful. Later on, however, it produces a harvest of righteousness and peace for those who have been trained by it."

- Hebrews 12:11 NIV

Affirmations:

I am financially disciplined. Self-discipline is key to my freedom.

I stay committed to following my budget. I will only say yes to the things I absolutely need.

I am disciplined and smart with how I spend my wealth. I never spend money impulsively.

I have the discipline to make hard financial choices now to enjoy an easy life later.

I daily apply wisdom with money.

AMEN.

I Pay
Attention To
My Finances!

"And he said to them, "Take care, and be on your guard against all covetousness, for one's life does not consist in the abundance of his possessions."

- Luke 12:15 ESV

Affirmations:

I give my finances great attention and care. I refuse to be careless about my finances.

I keep track of my finances, ensuring that I don't spend more than I earn. I am becoming more financially healthy.

I am in total control of my money. My money does not control me.

Each day, my financial situation gets better and better. I enjoy financial stability and prosperity.

AMEN.

I Am In Control Of My Expenses!

"The plans of the diligent lead surely to abundance and advantage. But everyone who acts in haste comes surely to poverty."

- Proverbs 21:5 AMP

Affirmations:

I am in control of my expenses. I watch my spending habits closely. I track my expenses.

I will only spend money on things that I need, and I overcome the urge to spend money on things that I do not need.

I plan my expenses wisely, and because of this, I have surplus money to invest and save.

My finance is on the right trajectory. I am completely in control of my expenses.

AMEN.

My Goals Are Materialising!

"But as for you, be strong and do not give up, for your work will be rewarded."

- 2 Chronicles 15:7 NIV

Affirmations:

I am achieving the financial goals
I have set. All my goals are
manifesting.

My short-, mid-, and long-term
goals are SMART – Specific,
Measurable, Achievable,
Realistic, and Timely.

I daily look unto Jesus to guide
my path as I pursue my goals. I
surround myself with
goal-oriented people.

God pours out extravagant grace
on me. My financial dreams are
materialising.

AMEN.

My God Is Jehovah Jireh!

"And Abraham called the name of that place Jehovah-Jireh: as it is said to this day, in the mount of Jehovah it shall be provided."

- Genesis 22:14 ASV

<u>Affirmations:</u>

I rejoice in the bountiful blessings from Jehovah Jireh. He is God my provider.

I exude passion, purpose, and prosperity. All my bills are paid with wonderful ease.

I am prosperous, wealthy, and happy. Prosperity and abundance come to me easily and effortlessly.

I call those things that be not as though they were. I call my financial freedom into existence.

AMEN.

All My Needs Are Met!

"And my God will supply every need of yours according to his riches in glory in Christ Jesus."

- Philippians 4:19 ESV

Affirmations:

I know my needs from my wants. I always have enough of all that I need and desire. All my needs are met.

The young lions sometimes go hungry, but because I trust in the Lord, I lack no good thing.

Jehovah Jireh supplies all my needs according to His riches in glory in Christ Jesus.

God has blessed me abundantly, so that in all things and at all times, having all that I need, I abound in every good work.

AMEN.

I Lack No Good Thing!

"The young lions lack food and grow hungry, but they who seek the Lord will not lack any good thing."

- Psalm 34:10 AMP

<u>Affirmations:</u>

Because I seek the Lord, I lack no good thing.

The Lord supplies all my needs according to His riches in glory through Christ Jesus.

I am becoming financially free with the help of God. I am on the road to financial success.

I am strong and courageous. I turn not to the right or the left. I am blessed wherever I go.

I prosper and I am in good health even as my soul prospers.

AMEN.

I Will Not Beg For Bread!

"I was young and now I am old, yet I have never seen the righteous forsaken or their children begging bread."

- Psalm 37:25 NIV

Affirmations:

I was young, now I am old, I have never seen the righteous forsaken or their children beg for bread. I will not beg for bread.

They that put their trust in the Lord shall know no shame. Shame is not my portion concerning my finances.

My finances are constantly improving despite any current challenges.

The Lord is working things out for my good. I enjoy financial stability and prosperity.

AMEN.

My Debts Are Settled!

"Owe no man any thing, but to love one another: for he that loveth another hath fulfilled the law."

- Romans 13:8 KJB

Affirmations:

All my bills are paid. All my debts
are settled.

My credit cards are now clear of
any balances. I am liberated.

My income exceeds my
expenses; I am debt free with
money to spend.

I am doing whatever it takes to
stay out of debt. I handle my
finances with care and attention.

I owe nothing to any man, except
for love. I am a Lender to nations
and not a Borrower.

AMEN.

Debt-Free Life Is Mine!

"When the Lord your God blesses you as He has promised you, then you will lend to many nations, but you will not borrow; and you will rule over many nations, but they will not rule over you."

- Deuteronomy 15:6 AMP

Affirmations:

I am committed and focused on getting out of debt. Debt-free living is mine to enjoy.

I make the necessary adjustment in my lifestyle so that I can live debt free. I owe nothing to any man, except for love.

I am capable of managing my debt. My debt will not spiral out of my control.

I will continue to live an abundant debt-free life. I am mindful of eliminating all debts from my life.

AMEN.

I Am Equipped With Financial Knowledge!

"By knowledge the rooms are filled with all precious and pleasant riches."

- Proverbs 24:4 ESV

Affirmations:

I am not ignorant about Financial Education. I am wiser every day as I develop my financial knowledge.

Financial podcasts and books teach me strategies to grow my wealth. I seek the advice from wise counsel.

I seek financial knowledge. I am willing to learn, unlearn, relearn, and grow.

I strive for progress, not perfection. Financial discipline is my freedom.

AMEN.

I Make Wise Spending Decisions!

"Wise people live in wealth and luxury, but stupid people spend their money as fast as they get it."

- Proverbs 21:20 GNT

Affirmations:

Spending decisions are mine to make. I know my needs from my wants.

I live below my means but within my needs. Living on less makes my life better.

When I spend money, I make more money, money never finishes in my hand.

I spend money in alignment with my Godly values. I am a prudent steward of God's financial blessings.

AMEN.

I Prioritise Savings!

"Lazy people should learn a lesson from the way ants live. They have no leader, chief, or ruler, but they store up their food during the summer, getting ready for winter."

- Proverbs 6:6-8 GNT

Affirmations:

I chose to prioritise savings; I have more than enough income to save for my future.

I pay myself first as a priority; I don't spend everything I earn.

My savings increases in the multiples; saving is an act of abundance for me.

My bank account keeps on growing bigger. My financial path shines brighter and brighter unto the perfect day.

AMEN.

I Have
Emergency
Fund!

"A prudent person foresees danger and takes precautions. The simpleton goes blindly on and suffers the consequences."

- Proverbs 27:12 (NLT)

Affirmations:

I am building an emergency fund to protect and safeguard myself.

I am great at consistently saving money. I am always finding more ways to save money.

I am always growing my savings and investments pot. I enjoy the challenge of saving more money.

My budgeting plan incorporates savings. My future self will thank me for saving money today.

With God's help, there are no limits to how much I can save.

AMEN.

"When you give to the poor, it is like lending to the Lord, and the Lord will pay you back."

- Proverbs 19:17 GNT

Affirmations:

I am a cheerful and generous giver. I help those in need. I open my hand with compassion.

The more money I have, the more money I give. What I give multiplies so I have even more to give. I rejoice in giving.

I choose to make an impact on the lives of those around me through my loving act of generosity.

I scatter and I increase more and more. I give in secret. The Lord rewards me openly.

AMEN.

I Am A Giver!

"Remember this: Whoever sows sparingly will also reap sparingly, and whoever sows generously will also reap generously. Each of you should give what you have decided in your heart to give, not reluctantly or under compulsion, for God loves a cheerful giver."

- 2 Corinthians 9:6-7 NIV

Affirmations:

I have God's nature of generosity. I am a great giver.

I have more than enough. I am blessed to be a blessing.

I tithe and give offerings regularly; I honour the Lord with my wealth.

I am known for my giving; I give generously to others without expecting a reward.

I give willingly to those in need and the Lord blesses everything that I do.

AMEN.

I Am Open To Receive!

"Give, and it will be given to you. They will pour into your lap a good measure, pressed down, shaken together, and running over. For with the standard of measurement you use when you do good to others, it will be measured to you in return."

- Luke 6:38 AMP

Affirmations:

I am open to receive. I receive monetary blessings in unique ways.

I am willing, ready, and able to receive financial blessings from others. I give generously and receive graciously.

I am grateful for what I already have and for all that I receive. Money comes to me from unexpected sources.

As I give, it is given to me, good measure, pressed down, shaken together, and running over.

AMEN.

I Am Rescued From My Past!

"Forget the former things. Do not dwell on the past. See, I am doing a new thing! Now it springs up; do you not perceive it? I am making a way in the wilderness and streams in the wasteland."

- Isaiah 43:18-19 NIV

Affirmations:

I forgive myself for my past poor money choices.

My past money mistakes do not define my future blessings.

My past money mistakes led me to my abundant present life.

I am rescued from my past. My financial future is secure in Christ.

Anything I have lost will be given back to me. The Lord is gracious towards me.

AMEN.

I Am A Doer Of God's Will!

"You need to be patient, in order to do the will of God and receive what He promises."

- Hebrews 10:36 GNT

Affirmations:

I experience financial success by listening to, and doing the will of God to the best of my ability.

I am successful and prosperous, for I obey the voice of the Lord.

I embrace true humility and fear of the Lord, which lead to riches, honour, and long life.

I experience success by avoiding the path of destruction. I walk in the way of the Lord.

AMEN.

PART 3:

'MULTIPLYING MONEY' AFFIRMATIONS

I Am Blessed!

"And God is able to bless you abundantly, so that in all things at all times, having all that you need, you will abound in every good work."

- 2 Corinthians 9:8 NIV

<u>Affirmations:</u>

I am blessed with everything money can buy and everything money can't buy.

I am blessed in the city. I am blessed in the field. I am blessed coming in. I am blessed going out.

The fruit of my labour is blessed. My basket and store are blessed. My wallet and bank account are blessed.

I am blessed beyond the curse. I have an abundance of all things.

AMEN.

I Have The Wisdom Of God!

"I will do what you have asked. I will give you more wisdom and understanding than anyone has ever had before or will ever have again."

- 1Kings 3:12 GNT

Affirmations:

I am filled with the wisdom of God. I make wise and prosperous financial decisions.

Wisdom and knowledge are granted to me. God gives me riches and wealth in abundance.

God is downloading knowledge, wisdom, and insights into my life. I bring solutions to the world's problems and make wealth thereby.

I am filled with the knowledge of God's will in all wisdom. His will is my prosperity.

AMEN.

My Earning Potential Is Limitless!

"And the man Isaac became great and gained more and more until he became very wealthy and extremely distinguished."

- Genesis 26:13 AMP

Affirmations:

My earning potential is limitless. I can see income opportunities everywhere.

My Income increases in the multiples. I am creating more and more wealth every day.

I welcome an unlimited source of income and wealth into my life. Money is abundant to me.

Lucrative wealth-making opportunities and resources are headed my way. God has given me the power to make wealth.

Amen.

I Have More Than Enough!

"And God is able to give you more than you need, so that you will always have all you need for yourselves and more than enough for every good cause."

- 2 Corinthians 9:8 GNT

Affirmations:

The Lord multiplies all my resources. I am increasing.

My wealth extends beyond money. God's blessings on me are more than enough.

Prosperity is overflowing my way. I enjoy prosperity and abundance.

I have enough money to create the life of my dreams. I do not worry about money.

AMEN.

I Receive Increase, Bonuses And Raises!

"A person who works is paid wages, but they are not regarded as a gift; they are something that has been earned."

- Romans 4:4 GNT

Affirmations:

I am open and receptive to unexpected financial bonuses. I receive increases, bonuses, and raises.

I receive exceedingly abundantly more than I can ask or think according to God's power in me.

I am handling great amounts of money successfully. The Lord's abundant riches have lifted me.

The wealth of the Gentiles has come to my light, and Kings to the brightness of my rising.

AMEN.

I Am On The Path To Great Wealth!

"Honor the Lord with your wealth And with the first fruits of all your crops (income). Then your barns will be abundantly filled. And your vats will overflow with new wine."

- Proverbs 3:9-10 AMP

Affirmations:

I am on the path to great wealth. Financial doors keep opening for me. I am a self-made millionaire.

Money is an abundant resource that I can earn. I am becoming richer every day.

When people say there is a casting down, my testimony will be that of a lifting up.

I am like a city built on the hills; my financial glory will continually shine. I declare that I am wealthy.

AMEN.

I Am Redeemed From Poverty!

"For you know the grace of our Lord Jesus Christ, that though he was rich, yet for your sake he became poor, so that you through his poverty might become rich."

- 2 Corinthians 8:9 NIV

<u>Affirmations:</u>

I am redeemed from poverty, lack, and want. I always have more than enough.

I have been made rich through the finished work of Jesus on the cross. He became poor so through His poverty I have become rich.

I have been redeemed and freed from the curse of the law - that includes the curse of poverty!

I am a child of God. I am part of the royal family. I have resources that flow to me continually.

AMEN.

I Am A Smart Investor!

"Invest in seven ventures, yes, in eight; you do not know what disaster may come upon the land."

- Ecclesiastes 11:2 NIV

<u>Affirmations:</u>

I am a smart Investor, dedicated to seeking smart investments.

I take calculated risks and have confidence in my decisions.

I am happy to find success in my investments. I am optimistic about all my financial decisions.

My income is increasing every day because of my wise investing decisions.

My investments allow me to live life to the full.

AMEN.

My Investments Bring Wealth!

"The man who had received five bags of gold went at once and put his money to work and gained five bags more. So also, the one with two bags of gold gained two more."

- Matthew 25:16-17 NIV

Affirmations:

The Lord guides my hands to profit. I am blessed.

Wise investments are building my wealth every day. My capacity to grow my money expands.

Taking risks opens new opportunities for me. Compound interest works in my favour.

I am a well-informed investor. My investments increase in the multiples.

AMEN.

1.

I Leave Financial Inheritance!

"A good man leaves an inheritance to his children's children."

- Proverbs 13:22 NKJV

Affirmations:

My work today is building generational wealth. I leave an inheritance for my children's children.

My children and seeds to come through them call me blessed. My financial abundance overflows.

The next generation after me will manage God's blessings God's way for God's glory long after I've graduated to heaven.

I build a portfolio of wealth. I am blessed to be a blessing.

AMEN.

My Trust Is In The Lord!

"Trust in the Lord with all your heart. Never rely on what you think you know. Remember the Lord in everything you do, and he will show you the right way."

- Proverbs 3:5-6 GNT

Affirmations:

My trust is in the Lord.
I am lavished with unfailing
abundance. I will not be shaken.

God daily loads me with His
benefits. He has brought me into
my wealthy place.

Because I trust in the name of
the Lord, my capacity is fully
enlarged. I always prosper in all
things.

I have unlimited financial
abundance. My supply is endless
and inexhaustible.

AMEN.

I Have The Mind Of Christ!

"For who has known the mind and purposes of the Lord, so as to instruct Him? But we have the mind of Christ to be guided by His thoughts and purposes."

- 1 Corinthians 2:16 AMP

Affirmations:

I have the mind of Christ; all things are possible for me.

There is enough for all, I have an abundance mindset.

I have a success and growth mindset. My mind is open to the infinite supply of wealth.

I think big and I act even bigger. My God is a Big God.

Like God, I see things that are not as though they already are. I call my prosperity into being.

AMEN.

My Thoughts Are Agreeable To God's Will!

"Teach me to do Your will so that I may please You. For You are my God. Let Your good Spirit lead me on level ground."

- Psalm 143:10 AMP

Affirmations:

God causes my thoughts to be agreeable to His will.

I take captive every thought of failure and defeat that might want to inhabit my mind.

I fill my mind with the idea of abundance. Abundance manifests in all my affairs.

I place my entire focus and thought on God as the only source of my prosperity.

My prosperity thoughts create unlimited prosperity for me.

AMEN.

There Is Hope
For My
Future!

"For I know the plans I have for you,"
declares the LORD, "plans to prosper
you and not to harm you, plans to
give you hope and a future."

- Jeremiah 29:11 NIV

Affirmations:

God has prospered me and given me hope and a future. I prosper wherever I turn.

I delight myself in the Lord and He gives me the desires of my heart.

I seek first God's Kingdom and His righteousness, and He gives me everything I need.

I am faithful in the little things; therefore, the Lord blesses me with big things. I am daily loaded with His benefits.

AMEN.

IN CLOSING

Congratulations! You've made it to the end of this book. I hope the powerful biblical money affirmations in this book have inspired you or anyone else trying to improve his or her financial situation, or just looking for some positive inspiration for their day.

Biblical affirmations for financial success and prosperity are powerful because they are the words of God. His words give you the courage to dream of things that you wouldn't have done otherwise. These words help you appreciate God's love for you and encourage you always to be grateful to Him. They give you hope and show you the light at the end of the tunnel. They give you the courage to carry on and to not give up amidst difficult challenges.

If you are looking for scriptural references to get all the good things in your life, look no further than the biblical affirmations for finances. You will get to understand that when you trust the Lord and walk righteously in the path that He has chosen for you, He will bless you with all the abundance you need.

I will not forget to stress the importance of putting your faith to work. These biblical affirmations for financial success and prosperity will only work for you if you are willing to manifest the same for yourself. Hard work, diligence, consistently labouring and putting into action good financial habits are crucial for achieving financial success. Until you faithfully do your part, mere affirmations will not bring abundance into your life. It's like having faith without work, in which the end result is dead (James 2:17). The Bible, through powerful affirmations, teaches you to seek the Lord in everything you do, and you will thereafter enjoy prosperity, success, wealth, and abundance.

I usually wrap up my books by talking about the importance of financial education. If this book is the first book on personal finance you've ever read, don't let it be the last. Read more books about money, keep learning, listen to podcasts, ask questions, attend financial literacy seminars, sign up for finance courses, seek knowledge, and make learning a habit.

Even if it's something small, try learning at least one new thing about money management every day. Be mindful of your continuing education. Go into the day having a specific goal in mind, or an area of personal finance in which you want to develop. By keeping in mind that you should always be learning, you'll easily continue your education and make strides toward the financial freedom and financial independence you yearn for!

ABOUT OYENIKE ADETOYE

Oyenike (also known as Nike) is an impactful speaker, author, and personal finance expert. A Chartered Management Accountant by profession, Nike founded LifTED Finance Consulting Ltd, a private financial firm that educates, coaches and supports people on their journey through financial fitness and wealth management.

Nike defines success by the number of lives impacted, changed, and empowered through her message of hope in the area of personal finance. Her book series: "NonSecrets of the Financially Secure", "Praying for your Finances", "Financial Nakedness", "Financially Smart Teens & Young Adults", "The Beauty of Compounding", "The Four Letter Word DEBT", "Financial Boundaries", and "Financial Success Quenchers", provides simple guiding principles that empower people to win with their money. She is happily married and blessed with two beautiful children.

Connect with Oyenike online:
W▶ http://www.liftedfinance.com/
E▶ info@liftedfinance.com
T▶ https://twitter.com/FinanceLifted
F▶ https://www.facebook.com/liftedfinanceconsultingltd/
I ▶ https://www.instagram.com/liftedfinance/
L▶ https://www.linkedin.com/company/liftedfinanceconsulting/

FINANCES
Biblical Affirmations

By: Oyenike Adetoye   ACMA, CGMA

"The Bible has many money affirmations, and I have picked just a few for you. All the affirmations from the scripture lead to one factor; to be grateful to the Lord and think of Him in every step you take."

— Oyenike Adetoye